CONTENTS

1 What is economics?

1 The diagram below shows the production possibility curve (PPC) curve for an economy.

  a Explain why the PPC is drawn as concave to the origin. [2]

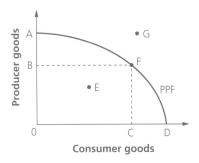

  b Outline the opportunity cost to the economy if it produces OC units of consumer goods. [2]

  c Explain which of the three points (E, F or G) indicates that the economy could increase output without incurring any opportunity costs. [2]

2 Growth in an economy can be shown diagrammatically by an outwards shift of the production possibility curve (PPC) for the economy. Explain **two** causes of the shift in the economy's PPC from PPC_1 to PPC_2 in the diagram below. [4]

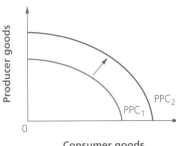

3 A dentist is currently paid an annual salary of $150,000. She is considering setting up her own dental clinic for which she expects to have potential revenues of $900,000 per year and annual total costs of $760,000.

   a Calculate the expected accounting profit if the dentist sets up her own clinic. [2]

   b Calculate the expected total economic profit if the dentist sets up her own clinic. [2]

   c Based on your calculations, outline whether the dentist should open her own clinic. [2]

4 Jen bought a smartphone for $600 last month but has never used it. The second-hand value of the smartphone is $420.

   a Explain the opportunity cost to Jen of owning the smartphone. [2]

   b Jen downloads freeware (software that is available for free download) onto her smartphone. Explain why the freeware is not an example of a free good in economics. [2]

5 The table below shows the production possibilities for a farmer.

Strawberries (kg)	Potatoes (kg)
320	860
340	800
360	740
380	680

a Calculate the opportunity cost of producing each extra 1 kg of strawberries for the farmer. [2]

b Calculate the opportunity cost to the farmer of increasing the production of potatoes from 740 kg to 800 kg. [2]

Unit 2 Microeconomics

2 Demand

1 The demand for organic free-range chicken has increased. However, the cost of supplying organic free-range chicken to supermarkets has also increased.

   a Define the term *demand*. [2]

   ....

   ....

   ....

   b Sketch a suitable demand diagram to show the impact on price following an increase in demand for organic free-range chicken. [2]

   c Sketch a suitable demand diagram to show the impact on price following an increase in the cost of supplying organic free-range chicken to supermarkets. [2]

2   The diagram below shows the market demand for Nike football boots (soccer shoes).

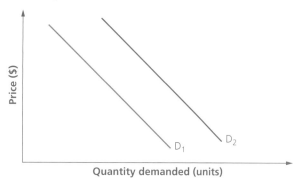

   a   Outline the difference between a movement along a demand curve and a shift in the demand curve for football boots.   [2]

....

....

....

....

   b   Explain **two** factors that may have caused the shift in the demand curve for football boots.   [4]

....

....

....

....

....

....

3   The table below shows the demand for cinema tickets at a local movie theatre. Quantities are expressed as the average number of tickets per week.

Price of tickets ($)	Adults (D₁)	Children (D₂)	Students (D₃)	Market demand (D₄)
10	4,700	3,500	2,600	
12	4,300	3,000	2,300	
14	3,900	2,500	2,000	
16	3,500	2,000	1,700	

   a   Define the term *market demand*.   [2]

....

....

....

b Use the table above to calculate the value of market demand for cinema tickets at each price level. [2]

....

....

c Use the table and your answer from Question **3a** to plot the individual demand curves (adults, children and students) and the market demand curve for cinema tickets. [3]

4 The diagram below shows the daily demand for a brand of ice cream in Paris for an average week in March.

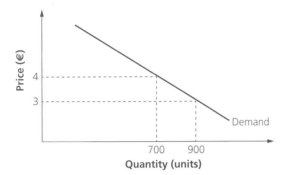

a Use the diagram to determine whether the firm should sell its ice cream at €3 or €4. [3]

....

....

....

b Explain the difference between a movement along a demand curve and a shift in the demand curve for ice cream. [4]

....

....

....

....

....

....

c Outline **one** reason why the demand for ice cream might be different during the month of August. [2]

....

....

....

....

....

5 Answer the following questions with reference to the demand curve shown below. (HL only)

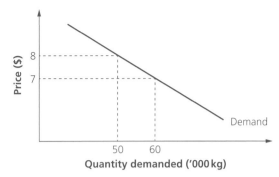

a Define the term *law of demand*. [2]

....

....

....

....

b With reference to the substitution and income effects, explain why the demand curve is downward sloping. [4]

....

....

....

....

....

....

....

c Calculate the change in the value of sales revenue if the firm raises its price from $7 to $8 and comment on your findings. [4]

....

....

....

....

....

....

3 Supply

1   The Emirates Stadium in north London has a seating capacity of 60,704.

   a   Define the term *supply*.   [2]

   ....

   ....

   ....

   ....

   b   Draw a supply curve to represent the situation at the Emirates Stadium.   [2]

   c   Explain the shape of the supply curve drawn for the Emirates Stadium.   [2]

   ....

   ....

   ....

   ....

2   The table below shows the supply of freshly made cookies at a local bakery. Quantities are expressed as the average number of cookies per week.

Price of cookies ($)	Chocolate chip (S₁)	Oatmeal (S₂)	Dark chocolate (S₃)	Market supply (S₄)
1	2,200	1,300	1,800	
2	2,500	1,400	2,000	
3	2,800	1,500	2,200	
4	3,100	1,600	2,400	

   a   Define the term *market supply*.   [2]

   ....

   ....

   ....

b Use the table above to calculate the value of market supply of cookies at each price level. [2]

....

....

....

c Use the table and your answer from Question **2b** to plot the individual supply curves (chocolate chip, oatmeal and dark chocolate) and the market supply curve for cookies. [3]

3 The supply curve below represents the market supply curve for electric cars in an economy, per time period.

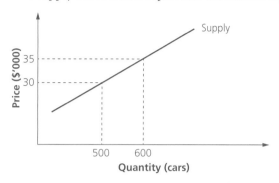

a Define the term *law of supply*. [2]

....

....

....

....

b With reference to the diagram above, explain the difference between a movement along a supply curve and a shift in the supply curve for electric cars. [4]

....

....

....

....

4 The chart below shows the number of IB Diploma candidates who took the Economics examination between 2005 and 2020.

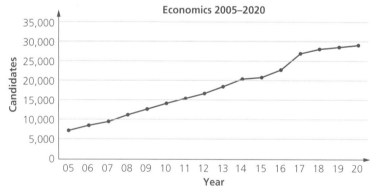

Explain **two** factors that might shift the market supply curve of IB Economics textbooks. [4]

....

....

....

....

....

5 Use an appropriate supply diagram to explain how the imposition of a tax on suppliers of oil (petrol) affects the quantity supplied. [4]

4 Competitive market equilibrium

1 The questions below refer to this diagram for a particular meal.

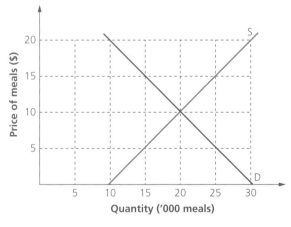

a Explain what is meant by *market equilibrium*. [2]

b Calculate the excess supply or excess demand if the price is $15. [2]

....

....

....

2 The diagram below represents the market for a particular toy.

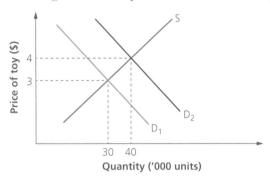

a Calculate the change in total revenue if the market demand curve shifts from D_1 to D_2. [2]

....

....

....

....

b State **two** possible reasons for the change in the market demand curve shown in the diagram. [2]

....

....

....

3 The diagram below represents the market for a textbook, for a given time period. (HL only)

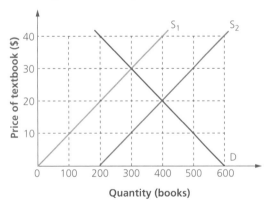

a Outline **two** possible reasons for the shift in the supply curve. [4]

....

....

....

....

b Calculate the change in the sales revenue of the textbook supplier following the change in the market equilibrium price.

[2]

c State the impact of an increase in supply on consumer surplus **and** producer surplus.

[2]

4 The table below shows the demand and supply schedules for a product. Suppose a fall in production costs increases supply by 20 units at each given price.

Price ($)	Quantity demanded (units)	Quantity supplied (units)
5	100	60
6	90	70
7	80	80
8	70	90

a Identify the original market equilibrium price.

[1]

b Calculate the new equilibrium price.

[2]

5 The table below shows the demand and supply schedules for a particular good, per time period. (HL only)

Price ($)	Quantity demanded (units)	Quantity supplied (units)
0	800	0
10	600	200
20	400	400
30	200	600
40	0	800

a Plot the demand and supply curves and identify the equilibrium price and equilibrium quantity. [4]

Equilibrium price ....

Equilibrium quantity ....

b Define the term *consumer surplus*. [2]

....

....

....

c   Use your answers from Question **5a** and Question **5b** to calculate the value of the consumer surplus at
the equilibrium price.   [2]

d   Calculate the shortage at a price of $10 per unit.   [2]

e   Calculate the quantity of excess supply at a price of $30 per unit.   [2]

5 Price elasticity of demand (PED)

1   A firm sells 200 units of its product each day at a price of $4, with a known price elasticity of demand (PED)
of −2.0.

a   Calculate the value of the firm's sales revenue.   [1]

b   Calculate the new sales revenue if the firm increases its price by 20%.   [2]

c   Explain whether raising its price was a good decision for the firm.   [2]

2   In the diagram below, point *x* represents the mid-point on the demand curve. (HL only)

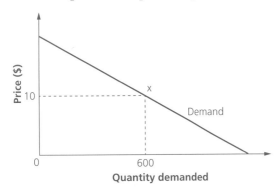

a   State the value of the price elasticity of demand (PED) at point *x*.   [1]

....

....

b   Explain what will happen to total revenue if the price falls below $10.   [2]

....

....

....

....

3   Refer to the data below for a given product and answer the following questions. (HL only)

Unit price (€)	15	25	40
Sales revenue (€)	300	500	800

a   Comment on the value of the price elasticity of demand (PED) for the product.   [2]

....

....

....

....

b Use the data in the table to draw an accurately labelled demand diagram to illustrate the value of PED. [2]

4 A jewellery firm reduces the price of its platinum earrings from $400 to $350 per unit, resulting in the quantity demanded rising from 25 units to 30 units per month.

   a Calculate the value of the price elasticity of demand (PED) for the earrings. [2]

b Comment on the result of your answer for Question **4a**.   [2]

....

....

....

....

c Explain why the PED for many primary commodities (such as metal ores) has a relatively low value, while the demand for manufactured products (such as jewellery) has a relatively high PED value.   [2]

....

....

....

....

5 Study the demand schedule below and answer the questions that follow. (HL only)

Price per unit ($)	Quantity demanded	Price per unit ($)	Quantity demanded
10	0	4	6
9	1	3	7
8	2	2	8
7	3	1	9
6	4	0	10
5	5		

a Plot the demand curve. [2]

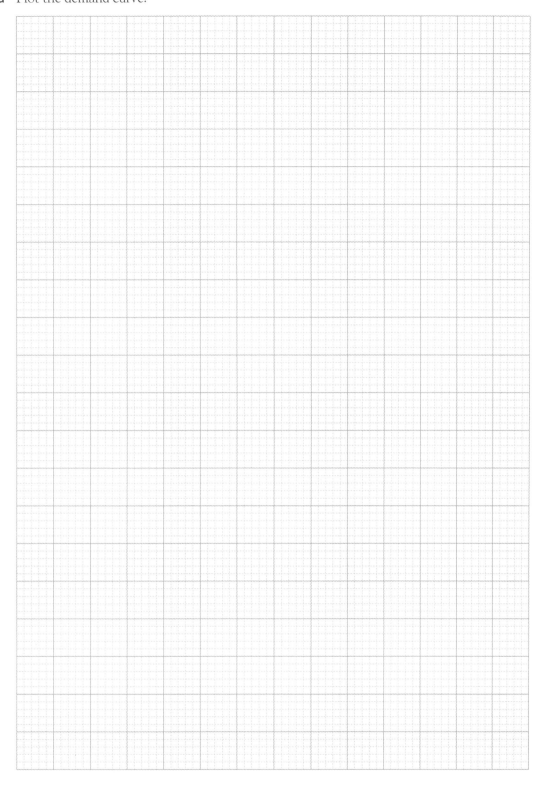

b Using a separate graph, plot the total revenue curve under the demand curve in Question **5a**. [3]

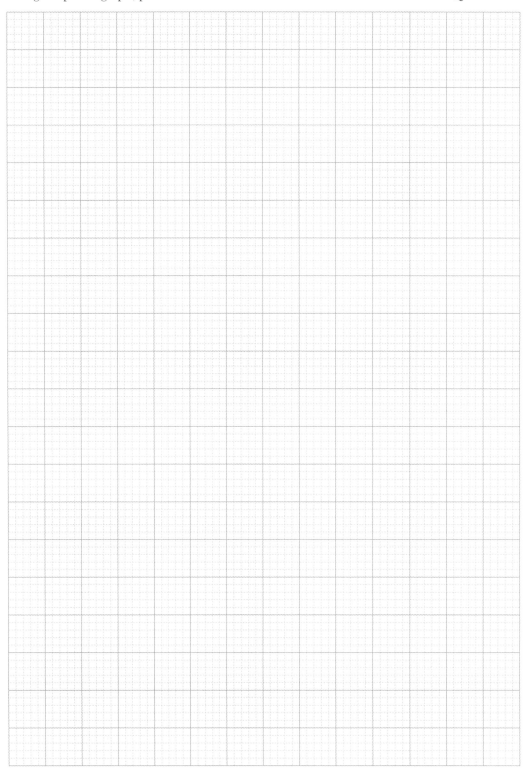

c   Using your understanding of the concept of price elasticity of demand (PED), explain why total revenue is maximized at the mid-point of a linear demand curve, i.e. at $5 in the above example. [3]

6 Income elasticity of demand (YED)

1   In the past year, average household income increased by 1%, and the inflation rate was 1.5%.

a   Outline **two** consequences (outcomes) from the above statement. [2]

b   Define the term *income elasticity of demand* (YED). [2]

c   Explain **two** ways that firms might be able to make use of estimates of YED for their products. [4]

2 a Calculate the income elasticity of demand (YED) for tea if a 3% increase in real household income causes sales of tea to rise from 100 million to 101 million units. [2]

....

....

....

....

b Comment on what this suggests about tea as a product. [2]

....

....

....

....

3 Assume the income elasticity of demand (YED) for cigarettes in a particular country is known to be +0.14.

a If there is a 3.5 per cent increase in real household income, explain what happens to the demand for cigarettes. [2]

....

....

....

....

b Using your answer from Question **3a**, briefly explain what the YED figure suggests about the demand for cigarettes in that country. [2]

....

....

....

....

c In the same country, the YED for potatoes is −0.35. Calculate the percentage change in the demand for potatoes, assuming all other things remain equal in the country. [2]

....

....

....

....

d Comment on your findings in Question **3c**. [2]

....

....

....

....

4 a Complete the diagrams below using Engel curves to show the relationship between household expenditure on a particular product and household income. [2]

b Explain whether the Engel curve diagram below shows income elastic or income inelastic demand for a particular product. [2]

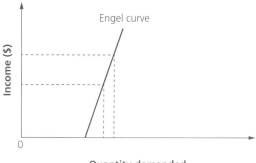

....

....

....

....

5 Study the estimates of income elasticity of demand (YED) for various products in a country then answer the questions that follow.

Product	YED (estimate)
Petrol (gas)	+0.25
Soft drinks	−0.33
Domestic holidays	+1.36
Public transport	−0.22

a Identify **one** inferior good and **one** luxury good from the products shown in the table. [2]

b Explain which suppliers of the above products would gain the most from an economic boom. [2]

c Explain which of the given suppliers would gain the most from an economic downturn (recession or slump). [2]

d If average household income increases by 3.5%, calculate the percentage change in the demand for public transport and domestic holidays. [3]

e Using the figures in the above table, explain why the government is more inclined to tax petrol rather than to tax providers of domestic holidays. [3]

7 Price elasticity of supply (PES)

1 a Calculate the value of the price elasticity of supply (PES) for Toyota motor vehicles from the diagram below, if price rises from $25,000 to $30,000.   [2]

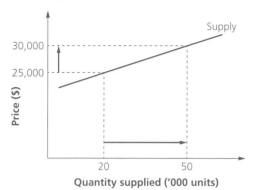

....

....

....

....

b Explain why a mass car manufacturer such as Toyota might have a high PES.   [2]

....

....

....

....

2 The data below refer to a local firm that sells hotdogs.

Price ($ per hotdog)	Quantity demanded (units)	Quantity supplied (units)
3	70	10
4	60	30
5	50	50
6	40	70
7	30	90

a Calculate the price elasticity of supply (PES) if price increases from $5 to $6 per hotdog.   [2]

....

....

....

....

b Comment on your answer to Question **2a** (the value of PES). [2]

c Suppose the government provides a subsidy that enables the hotdog retailer to increase the level of output by 30 units at all price levels. Plot a suitable diagram to determine the new equilibrium price and quantity. [3]

3 *Angry Birds* is a highly popular video game created by Finnish company Rovio, with more than 12 million customers having paid $0.99 each to download the game from Apple's App Store. With the use of an appropriate diagram, explain why the high level of demand for *Angry Birds* games has no direct effect on the selling price. [4]

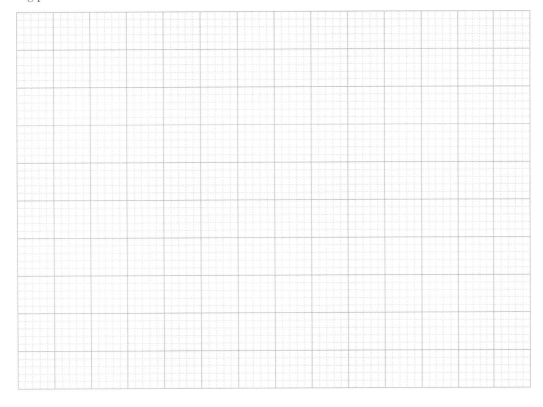

....

....

....

....

....

4 The supply curve for a particular Chanel handbag is shown in the diagram below.

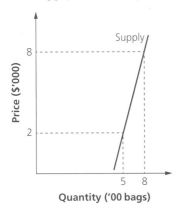

a State the intended sales of Chanel handbags at a unit price of $2,000. [1]

....

....

b Calculate the value of PES for Chanel handbags if the price quadruples from $2,000 to $8,000. [2]

c With reference to the diagram, explain why luxury handbags made by Chanel have a steep supply curve. [3]

5 a Explain whether the price elasticity of supply (PES) for oil (petroleum) is likely to be price elastic or price inelastic in the short run. [2]

b Explain whether the value of PES for oil (petroleum) is likely to increase over a longer time period. [2]

c Explain why the PES of commonly prescribed medicines is likely to be highly price elastic. [2]

8 Role of government in microeconomics

1 The table below shows the demand and supply schedules for Product Y. (HL only)

Demand	Price ($)	Supply
30,000	10	12,000
25,000	15	16,000
20,000	20	20,000
15,000	25	24,000
10,000	30	28,000
5,000	35	32,000

    a Identify the equilibrium price of Product Y. [1]

    b Define the term *price ceiling*. [2]

    c Briefly explain the impact of the government imposing a price floor of $25 for Product Y. [2]

2 The table below shows the demand (Qd) and supply (Qs) schedules for Product X. (HL only)

Qd	Price ($)	Qs
3,000	7	9,000
4,000	6	8,000
5,000	5	7,000
6,000	4	6,000
7,000	3	5,000
8,000	2	4,000
9,000	1	3,000

    a Identify the equilibrium price of Product X. [1]

    b State the amount of excess supply at a price of $5 per unit. [1]

c   Assume that the government imposes a specific tax of $2 per unit on Product X. Calculate the new equilibrium price.   [2]

d   Calculate the total tax revenue payable to the government.   [2]

e   Outline how much of the tax incidence is borne by the consumer.   [2]

3   The table below shows the demand (Qd) and supply (Qs) schedules for Product Z. (HL only)

Qd	Price ($)	Qs
30,000	7.5	90,000
40,000	7.0	80,000
50,000	6.5	70,000
60,000	6.0	60,000
70,000	5.5	50,000
80,000	5.0	40,000
90,000	4.5	30,000

a   Identify the equilibrium price and quantity for Product Z.   [2]

b   Suppose the government grants a subsidy of $1 per unit to the producers of Product Z. Calculate the new equilibrium price and quantity.   [3]

c Calculate the total cost to the government of passing the subsidy to producers of Product Z. [2]

....

....

....

d Calculate the value of the incidence of the subsidy that is passed on to consumers of Product Z. [2]

....

....

....

....

4 Refer to the graph below and answer the questions that follow. (HL only)

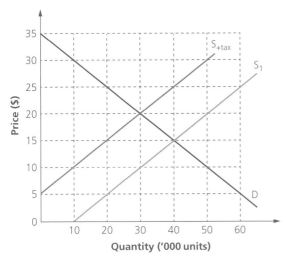

a Calculate the total tax revenue collected by the government from the imposition of the tax. [2]

....

....

....

b Calculate the incidence of tax paid by the consumer. [2]

....

....

....

c Calculate the change in consumer spending following the imposition of the tax. [2]

....

....

....

d Calculate the welfare loss resulting from the imposition of the tax. [2]

....

....

....

e Calculate the value of the producer surplus after the imposition of the tax. [2]

....

....

....

f Calculate the change in the value of consumer surplus after the tax has been imposed. [2]

....

....

....

5 Refer to the diagram below and answer the questions that follow. (HL only)

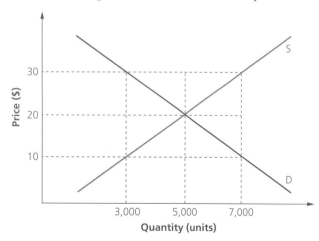

a Explain what situation arises if the government imposes a price floor of $30 for the product. [2]

....

....

....

....

b Calculate the change in consumer spending following the imposition of the price floor. [2]

....

....

....

....

....

....

c Calculate the change in producer revenue following the imposition of the price floor if the government buys all the surplus. [2]

....

....

....

....

....

....

d Suppose the government exports all the excess supply at $20 per unit. Calculate the amount of taxpayers' money needed to support this price control scheme. [2]

....

....

....

....

9 Market failure – externalities (externalities and common pool or common access resources)

1 The diagram below shows the before and after situation following the imposition of an indirect tax on cigarettes.

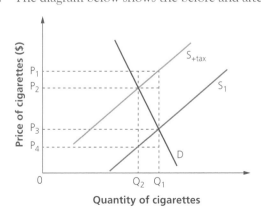

a   Identify the original equilibrium price and quantity.   [1]

....

b   Determine the amount of tax paid by smokers.   [2]

....

....

....

....

c   Determine the amount of tax revenue collected by the government.   [2]

....

....

....

....

d   Explain why the government might choose to tax the production and/or consumption of cigarettes.   [2]

....

....

....

....

2   The diagram below shows the market for tradable permits in Country X.

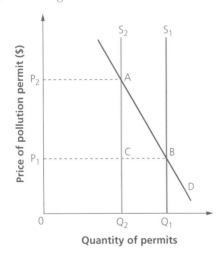

a With reference to the diagram above, explain the intended consequences following the decision to reduce the number of tradable permits in Country X. [4]

....

....

....

....

....

....

b Determine the change in the amount of revenue collected by the government after the reduction in the number of permits issued. [2]

....

....

....

3 Refer to the diagram below which represents the market for petrol (gas) in Country H prior to government intervention, where MPC = marginal private cost, and MPB = marginal private benefit.

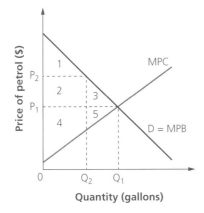

a State the area of consumer surplus without government intervention. [1]

....

b State the area of producer surplus without government intervention. [1]

....

c Suppose the government imposes a per unit carbon tax, causing the equilibrium price to rise to P_2. Draw the marginal social cost (MSC) curve on the diagram above and explain what happens to the value of consumer surplus. [3]

....

....

....

4 Petrol (gasoline) and cigarettes are examples of economic goods with negative externalities of consumption. (HL only)

   a Explain why negative externalities are an example of market failure. [2]

....

....

....

....

   b Apart from petrol (gas) and cigarettes, describe an example of a product with negative externalities. [2]

....

....

....

   c The diagram below shows the situation for the production of a demerit good.

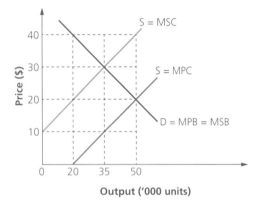

     i Identify the price and level of output in a market without government intervention. [1]

....

    ii Identify the socially optimal level of output and the price charged. [1]

....

....

  iii Calculate the value of the welfare gain if the economy reduced the production of the demerit good to the socially optimal level of output. [2]

....

....

....

5 The diagram below represents the situation for the consumption of junk food, a demerit good, which creates negative externalities of consumption.

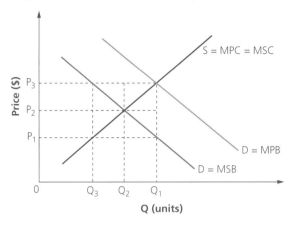

a Define the term *demerit good*. [2]

b Show on the diagram above the value of the negative externality of consumption of junk food. [1]
c Explain your answer to Question **5b**. [2]

10 Market failure – market power: perfect competition (HL only)

1 Answer the following questions, with reference to the diagram below, for a profit-maximizing firm operating under the conditions of perfect competition.

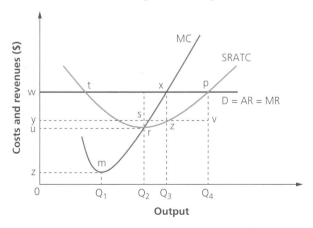

a Explain which level of output represents profit maximization for the firm. [2]

b Explain which level of output is the most economically efficient. [2]

c With reference to the diagram, explain whether the profit-maximizing firm earns economic profit. [2]

2 a Using an appropriate diagram, explain the short run loss position of a firm in perfect competition. [4]

....

....

....

....

....

....

b Use an appropriate diagram to explain why perfectly competitive firms can only earn normal profits in
the long run. [4]

....

....

....

....

....

3 a Explain the break-even price for a profit-maximizing firm with the following cost structure: average total
cost = $2.50 and the average variable cost = $2.00. [2]

....

....

....

b Explain the lowest price that the firm must charge **and** the break-even price for a profit-maximizing firm with the following revenue and cost structures: average revenue = \$35, and average variable cost = \$30. [4]

4 The diagram below shows the short run position for a firm operating in perfect competition.

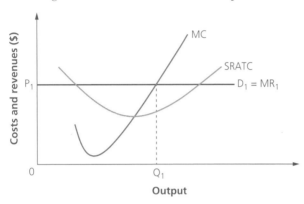

a On the diagram, show the profit or loss of the profit-maximizing firm. [1]

b On the diagram, show and explain the long run position of the profit-maximizing firm. [4]

5 The following questions refer to the diagram below.

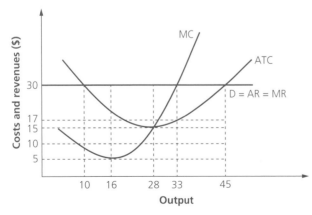

a With reference to the graph, identify the following:

   i The price charged in the long run. [1]

    ii The profit-maximizing level of output.   [1]

    iii The price that enables economic efficiency to occur.   [1]

b Calculate the value of the profit or loss of the profit-maximizing firm as shown in the diagram above.   [2]

c Suppose the current market price drops to $10. Explain what would happen in the long run.   [2]

d Calculate the value of the firm's normal profit in the long run.   [2]

11 Market failure – market power: monopoly (HL only)

1 Monopolies exist in all modern societies and can bring both benefits and disadvantages for the economy.

    a Define the term *monopoly*.   [2]

    b A profit-maximizing monopolist has the following cost and revenue structures in the short run. All monetary figures are in US dollars ($). Use the data to explain why the firm is not operating in a perfectly competitive market.   [2]

Output	Price	MR	MC	AC
150,000	15	5	5	9

c Calculate the value of abnormal profit earned by the monopolist. [2]

....

....

....

....

2 Refer to the diagram below and answer the questions that follow.

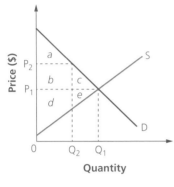

a State the area of consumer surplus in a competitive market. [1]

....

b State the area of producer surplus in a competitive market. [1]

....

c A monopolist opts to reduce the supply to Q_2 thereby forcing the price to rise to P_2. Identify the new consumer surplus and the new producer surplus. [2]

....

....

d Determine the loss in social (community) surplus following the decision by the monopolist to restrict supply from Q_1 to Q_2. [2]

....

....

3 Study the monopoly diagram below and answer the questions that follow.

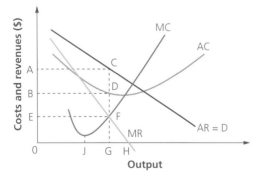

a Explain the price charged by a profit-maximizing monopolist. [2]

....

....

....

b Explain the total cost for the profit-maximizing monopolist. [2]

....

....

....

c Use the diagram to explain the amount of profit earned by the profit-maximizing monopolist. [2]

....

....

....

d Explain the level of output if the monopolist aims for revenue maximization. [2]

....

....

....

e Use the diagram to explain why the profit-maximizing monopolist is allocatively inefficient. [3]

....

....

....

4 The table below shows part of the demand schedule and cost structure for a profit-maximizing monopolist.

Quantity (units)	Price ($ per unit)	Total cost ($)	Total revenue ($)	Marginal revenue ($)	Marginal cost ($)
50	1,700	60,000			
60	1,600	68,000			
70	1,500	77,000			
80	1,400	87,000			
90	1,300	98,000			

a Complete the table above and determine the level of output for the monopolist. [4]

b Calculate the profit earned by the monopolist. [2]

5 Refer to the monopoly diagram below and answer the questions that follow.

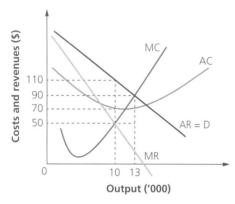

a Calculate the total revenue of the profit-maximizing monopolist. [2]

b Calculate the monopolist's total costs. [2]

c Determine the abnormal profit earned by the monopolist. [2]

d Calculate the welfare loss to society caused by the actions of the profit-maximizing monopolist. [2]

PHOTOCOPYING PROHIBITED

12 Market failure – market power: oligopoly (HL only)

1 Refer to the demand diagram below that represents collusive oligopoly acting as a monopoly.

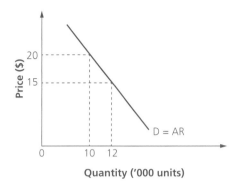

a Calculate the price elasticity of demand (PED) for the collusive oligopoly's product if firms in the industry simultaneously raise price from \$15 to \$20. [2]

....

....

....

b Calculate the collusive oligopoly's marginal revenue per unit if it increases output from 10,000 units to 12,000 units. [2]

....

....

....

c The diagram below represents the position of the collusive oligopoly acting as a monopoly.

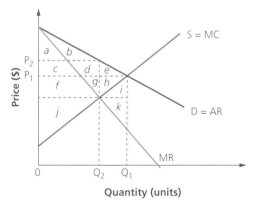

   i Identify the profit-maximizing level of output in the collusive oligopoly. [1]

....

   ii Identify the amount of producer surplus in the collusive oligopoly. [1]

....

iii With reference to the above diagram, explain why the collusive oligopoly acting as a monopoly worsens income distribution in the market. [2]

....

....

....

2 The data below shows the sales revenue for a particular industry.

Firm A	Firm B	Firm C	Firm D	Firm E
$2.5bn	$3.5bn	$2.7bn	$3.5bn	$3.8bn

a Calculate the 3-firm concentration ratio. [2]

....

....

....

....

b Comment on whether the industry is highly concentrated. [2]

....

....

....

....

....

3 Refer to the game theory information below for Adidas and Nike.

a Define the term *game theory*. [2]

....

....

....

b Explain what the dominant strategy would be for the two oligopolistic firms. [2]

....

....

....

c Explain why the sub-optimal result for non-collusive oligopolies (Decision D) is the most probable outcome in the long run. [2]

....

....

....

....

4 The diagram below represents a situation of collusive oligopoly.

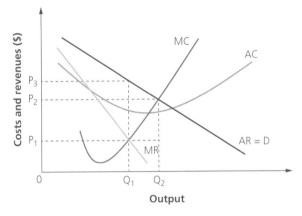

a Define the term *collusive oligopoly*. [2]

....

....

....

....

b With reference to the diagram, explain the equilibrium position of the oligopolistic firm. [2]

....

....

....

....

5 The diagrams below show the industry and an individual firm operating under an oligopolistic market structure consisting of three firms.

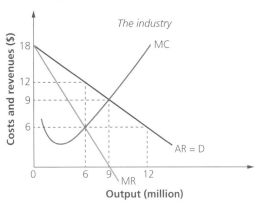 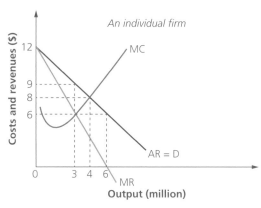

a   Identify the total output in the industry. [1]

b   If all firms in the industry agree to form a cartel, state the amount of output for the individual oligopolist if industry output is shared equally. [1]

c   Identify the price charged by each oligopolist firm operating in the cartel. [1]

d   Calculate the amount of revenue for each firm in the cartel. [2]

e   Identify the individual firm's profit-maximizing level of output. [1]

f   Show, using the data, why individual oligopolist firms are likely to be tempted to break this collusive agreement. [2]

13 Market failure – market power: monopolistic competition (HL only)

1 A profit-maximizing firm in monopolistic competition has the following costs and revenues.

Output (Q)	Total fixed costs ($)	Total revenue ($)	Average variable cost ($)
800	5,000	12,800	5.75

a Calculate the firm's average total cost. [2]

....

....

....

b Calculate the profit or loss made by the monopolistically competitive firm in the short run. [2]

....

....

....

....

2 The data below applies to a firm operating in monopolistic competition in the short run. All monetary figures are in US dollars ($).

MR	AR	MC	ATC
9	14	6	12

a Explain whether it would be financially beneficial for the monopolistically competitive firm to increase or reduce output. [2]

....

....

....

b Calculate the amount of profit or loss if the monopolistically competitive firm sells 6,000 units of output. [2]

....

....

....

3 The diagram below represents the short run position for a firm in monopolistic competition.

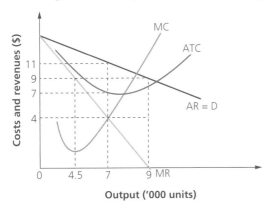

a State the level of output that the monopolistically competitive firm will operate at in the short run. [1]

....

b Calculate the profit or loss made by the monopolistically competitive firm in the short run. [2]

....

....

....

....

c Explain what is likely to happen to the value of profits for the firm in the long run. [2]

....

....

....

....

4 The diagram below shows the short run position for a profit-maximizing firm operating in a monopolistically competitive industry.

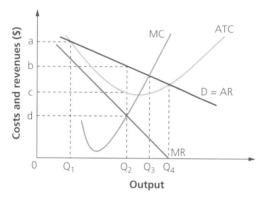

a Identify the level of output for the monopolistically competitive firm. [1]

....

b Identify the price charged by the firm in the short run. [1]

....

c Identify the per unit profit earned by the firm in the short run. [1]

....

d Explain what is likely to happen to the monopolistically competitive firm in the long run. [2]

....

....

....

....

5 The diagram below represents the short run position for a profit-maximizing firm operating under the conditions of monopolistic competition.

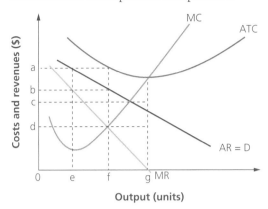

a State the level of output where the firm maximizes profit. [1]

b State the level of output where the firm maximizes total revenues. [1]

c State the area that represents the economic loss made by the firm. [1]

d On the diagram above, draw the average revenue curve in the long run for the monopolistically competitive firm. Label the new curve $AR_2 = D_2$ and explain your answer. [3]

14 Market failure – market power: rational producer behaviour (HL only)

1 A firm has annual fixed costs of $10 million. It has an annual output of 22,000 units and average variable cost of $120.

a Calculate the total cost for the firm. [2]

b If the firm charges a price of $800, calculate the annual profit made if it manages to sell all of its output. [2]

c Calculate the difference in the average cost of production at 11,000 units of output and at 22,000 units of output. [2]

....

....

....

....

d Explain what the figures in your answer to Question 1c suggest. [2]

....

....

....

....

2 The table below shows the total costs of production for STC Inc.

Output (kg)	Total costs ($)
0	15,000
50	25,000
100	33,000
150	39,000

a State the value of STC Inc.'s fixed costs. [1]

....

b Calculate the value of STC Inc.'s average variable cost if it produces 100 kg of output. [2]

....

....

c With reference to the data in the table, explain whether STC Inc. experiences economies of scale as it increases output from 50 kg to 150 kg. [3]

....

....

....

....

....

....

....

....

3 The table below shows SIS Ltd's total costs of production at various levels of output.

Output (kg)	Total costs ($)	Average costs ($)
0	200	
10	280	
20	480	
30	690	
40	900	

a Calculate the average cost of production and comment on whether SIS Ltd experiences economies of scale. [3]

b Calculate the value of the average fixed cost (AFC) of producing 20 kg of output. [2]

c Calculate the value of the AFC at the economic efficient level of output. [2]

d Calculate the value of the average variable cost (AVC) of producing 30 kg of output. [2]

4 The table below shows the cost of production for KGV Co. at various levels of output.

Output	Average fixed costs ($)	Total variable costs ($)
10	50	50
20	25	80
25	20	100

a Calculate the total fixed costs (TFC) of production for the firm. [1]

b Calculate the value of the average fixed cost if the firm produces 5 units of output. [2]

c Calculate the value of the average total cost if KGV Co. produces 25 units of output. [2]

d Calculate the marginal cost (MC) per unit if KGV Co. increases output from 10 to 20 units of output. [2]

5 The following data refer to the costs and revenues of RCHK & Co. when operating at 300 units of output per month.

Item	Costs and revenues ($)
Price	50
Raw materials per unit	15
Advertising costs	200
Rent	3,500
Salaries	3,000

a Explain why advertising costs are an example of fixed cost of production for RCHK & Co. [2]

b Calculate RCHK & Co.'s monthly total fixed costs of production. [2]

c Calculate RCHK & Co.'s total cost of producing 300 units. [2]

d Calculate the profit made by RCHK & Co. if the firm is able to sell all of its output. [2]

15 Measuring economic activity and illustrating its variations

1 a Define the term *gross national income* (GNI). [2]

....

....

....

....

b Calculate the value of gross domestic product (GDP) **and** gross national income (GNI) from the given information: Consumption = $150bn, Investment expenditure = $60bn, Government spending = $55bn, Export earnings = $31bn, Import expenditures = $28bn, Net property income from abroad = −$8bn. [3]

....

....

....

....

....

....

....

2 The data below are for Country G.

Year	Nominal GDP ($bn)	GDP deflator
2019	228.0	106.0
2020	230.2	107.8
2021	232.4	109.8

a Calculate the real GDP for Country G in 2020. [2]

....

....

....

b In Country G, the average annual salary in 2021 was $28,000. Calculate the average real income for the average worker in Country G. [2]

....

....

....

c Explain why, despite the nominal GDP increasing during the given time period, the real value of GDP in Country G had actually fallen.

[3]

3 The following list shows the total expenditures in Country C for last year. All monetary values are in billions of euros (€bn), expressed in current prices:

- Export earnings   = 96
- Government expenditure   = 195
- Household consumption   = 363
- Import expenditure   = 123
- Net property income   = 58
- Private-sector investments = 159

a Define the term *GDP at current prices*.

[2]

b Calculate the nominal value GDP for Country C.

[2]

c Calculate the real GDP for Country C if the GDP deflator for last year was 103.8.

[2]

d Country C's real GDP is €650.25 billion this year. Calculate the country's growth rate since last year.

[2]

4 The data in the table below refers to Country S in 2020 and 2021. All figures are in billions of US dollars.

Item	2020	2021
Consumption	80	85
Export receipts	35	40
Government spending	30	33
Import payments	40	36
Interest, profits and dividends	10	12
Investment	40	38
Wages and salaries	50	55

a Use the expenditure approach to calculate the nominal value of GDP for Country S in 2020. [2]

b Calculate the rate of economic growth in Country S in 2021. [3]

c Explain **two** limitations of using nominal GDP per capita as a measurement of the level of economic activity in Country S. [4]

5 The following information relates to Country K's gross domestic product (GDP) for last year.

Item of expenditure	Value of expenditure ($bn)
Consumption	231
Exports	24
Government	98
Imports	37
Investment	148
Savings	88
Taxation	112

a Calculate the value of Country K's gross domestic product. [2]

b Calculate the value of Country K's injections for last year. [2]

c Use the information to explain if Country K is contracting or expanding. [3]

d Determine the value of withdrawals in Country K necessary for national income equilibrium in the economy. [1]

e Explain whether Country K has a budget deficit or budget surplus. [2]

f Calculate Country K's external deficit as a percentage if its GDP. [2]

16 Variations in economic activity – aggregate demand and aggregate supply

1 Refer to the diagram below and answer the questions that follow.

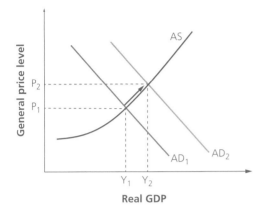

a Explain why the aggregate demand (AD) curve slopes downwards. [2]

b With reference to the diagram above, explain **two** possible reasons for the shift in an economy's aggregate demand curve from AD₁ to AD₂. [4]

2 Study the diagram below and answer the following questions.

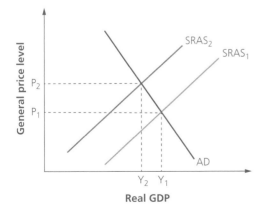

a   Define the term *short run aggregate supply* (SRAS).   [2]

b   Explain **two** possible causes of the shift in the short run aggregate supply (SRAS) curve from $SRAS_1$ to $SRAS_2$.   [2]

3 a   Define the term *long run aggregate supply* (LRAS).   [2]

b   With the aid of a suitable diagram, explain the shape of the long run aggregate supply (LRAS) curve according to neoclassical economists and monetarists.   [4]

4 Study the diagram below and answer the questions that follow.

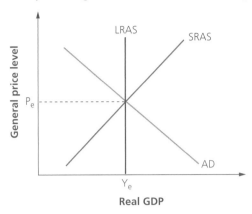

a Point Y_e represents the real national output level that corresponds with full employment in the economy. Define the term *full employment*. [2]

....

....

....

b Explain the level of real national output that represents long run equilibrium according to neoclassical economists. [2]

....

....

....

c Explain how higher interest rates in the economy are likely to cause a deflationary gap, and show this on the diagram above. [3]

....

....

....

....

....

....

5 Use the diagram below to answer the questions that follow.

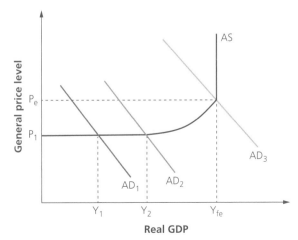

a Explain the likely impact on the economy if aggregate demand increases from AD_1 to AD_2. [2]

b If the economy is operating at Y_2, explain why it experiences a recessionary (negative output) gap. [2]

c Explain why an increase in aggregate demand beyond AD_3 will cause an inflationary gap. [2]

17 Macroeconomic objectives – economic growth

1 The data below show the nominal gross domestic product (GDP) for Country Y.

Year	Nominal GDP ($bn)	GDP deflator
2019	115.0	100.0
2020	118.6	103.2
2021	122.8	105.5

a Calculate the real GDP in 2020. [2]

b Calculate the nominal growth rate in 2020. [2]

c Explain what happened to real GDP between 2019 and 2020. [2]

d Calculate the real growth rate in 2021. [2]

....

....

....

2 The data below refer to Country W.

Year	Nominal GDP ($bn)	GDP deflator
2018	250	102.2
2019	260	100.0
2020	280	105.4
2021	320	108.6

a Calculate the real GDP for 2020. [2]

....

....

....

b Calculate the change in the real GDP between 2018 and 2019 and comment on your findings. [3]

....

....

....

c Suppose the population in Country W was 62 million in 2021. Calculate the nominal GDP per capita during the year. [2]

....

....

....

3 The chart below shows the nominal gross domestic product for Vietnam over a 5-year period.

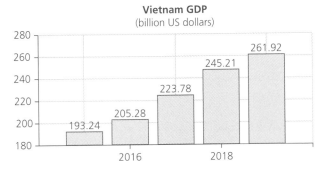

Vietnam GDP
(billion US dollars)

193.24 205.28 223.78 245.21 261.92

2016   2018

a Define the term *nominal gross domestic product.*   [2]

....

....

....

b Determine the year in which Vietnam experienced its highest gain in nominal GDP over the period shown.   [2]

....

....

....

c Determine the year in which economic growth was at its highest (round figures to 2 decimal places).   [2]

....

....

....

....

4 Study the following data for Country E and answer the questions below.

Economic variable	2020 ($bn)	2021 ($bn)
Capital consumption	7	9
Consumption	85	90
Export earnings	32	30
Government spending	38	38
Import expenditure	28	32
Interest, profit and dividends	9	7
Investments	30	35

a Using the expenditure approach, calculate the nominal value of Country E's gross domestic product (GDP) in 2020 and in 2021.   [3]

....

....

....

....

b Calculate the economic growth rate in Country E between 2020 and 2021.   [2]

....

....

....

c In Country E, the inflation index in 2020 was 102.5 and 107.6 in 2021. Calculate the value of Country E's real GDP in 2021. [2]

5 Complete the information in the table below by calculating the missing data for Country X. [5]

Year	Nominal GDP ($bn)	GDP deflator	Real GDP ($bn)	Nominal growth rate (%)	Real Growth rate (%)
2019	a	100.0	120.00	–	–
2020	126.5	102.8	b	5.41	c
2021	136.2	d	128.00	e	4.02

18 Macroeconomic objectives – low unemployment

1 Study the data below for Country X and answer the questions that follow.

Total population	80 million
Percentage of population employed	76.2%
Population of unemployed	8.2 million
Dependent population	13.55%

a Calculate the unemployment rate for Country X. [2]

b Suppose in the subsequent time period, 2 million immigrants enter Country X and all find employment. Calculate the new unemployment rate in Country X. [2]

2 The population data below is for Country Y, where the school leaving age is 16 and the retirement age is 67. The unemployment rate is reported to be 6%.

- Population = 66 million
- Age 0–15 = 12 million
- Age 16–66 = 38 million
- Age ≥67 = 16 million

a Define the term *unemployment rate*. [2]

b Calculate the number of people unemployed in Country Y. [2]

3 The following table shows employment data for Country Z.

Year	Population of working age	Active labour force
2019	20.9m	18.6m
2020	21.2m	18.8m
2021	21.6m	18.9m

a Outline the difference between Country Z's population of working age and the country's active labour force. [2]

b Calculate the number of people unemployed in Country Z in 2019 and 2021 if the unemployment rate was 5% and 5.45% respectively. [3]

c Explain why the unemployment rate in 2021 was higher than in 2020 despite there being an extra 100,000 people in the active labour force. [2]

4 The diagram below shows production possibility curves for Country A.

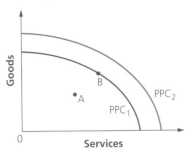

a Explain how the economy might move from point A to point B.　[2]

....

....

....

....

b Identify **two** possible causes of the shift in the production possibility curve from PPC_1 to PPC_2.　[2]

....

....

....

....

5 Use the data below for Country B to answer the following questions.

Labour market figures	
Total population	135.36 million
Adult population	94.00 million
Number of unemployed	10.81 million
Number employed	62.35 million

a Calculate the size of Country B's labour force.　[2]

....

....

....

b Calculate the labour force participation rate for Country B.　[2]

....

....

....

c Calculate the rate of unemployment in Country B.　[2]

....

....

....

19 Macroeconomic objectives – low and stable rate of inflation

1   Use the data below to calculate the weighted price index for Country W. (HL only)   [2]

Item of expenditure	This year's price index	Statistical weighting	Weighted price index
Housing	155.3	0.305	
Food	113.4	0.250	
Travel	125.2	0.225	
Clothing	131.6	0.115	
Entertainment	142.5	0.105	

2   The data below show the inflation rate in the United Arab Emirates between 2016 and 2021.

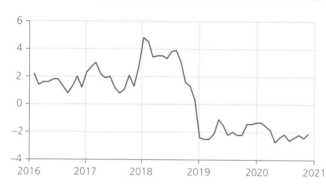

Outline what has happened to inflation in the United Arab Emirates during this time.   [2]

....

....

....

....

3   Refer to the data in the table below for Country X, which show the per unit prices of various products.

Year	Price of cinema tickets	Price of petrol	Price of poultry	Price of coffee
1	$15.00	$0.75	$6.00	$4.55
2	$13.50	$0.65	$6.50	$4.60

Explain why there is likely to have been deflation in Country X.   [4]

....

....

....

....

....

....

4 The table below shows the prices of four products in Country Y over a three-year period. (HL only)

Year	Price of alphas	Price of betas	Price of gammas	Price of deltas
1	$4.00	$4.90	$6.00	$5.00
2	$4.00	$5.20	$6.10	$5.30
3	$4.50	$5.50	$6.50	$5.50

The typical household basket of products contains 5 units of alphas, 3 units of betas, 2 units of gammas and 4 units of deltas.

a Use the table below to construct a weighted price index for Country Y, using Year 2 as the base year. [4]

Year	Spending on alphas	Spending on betas	Spending on gammas	Spending on deltas	Total cost of basket	Weighted index
1						
2						
3						

b Determine the inflation rate in Year 3. [1]

....

c Calculate the inflation rate in Year 2. [2]

....

....

....

5 The data below are for Country Z. (HL only)

Item	Consumer price index	Weight
Clothing	120	15
Food	130	30
Housing	140	40
Others	125	15

a Define the term *consumer price index* (CPI). [2]

....

....

....

b 'The typical household in Country Z spends more money on food than on clothing.'
Explain this statement. [2]

....

....

....

c Using the data above, calculate the weighted consumer price index (CPI) in Country Z. [2]

Item	CPI	Weight	Weighted CPI
Clothing	120	15	
Food	130	30	
Housing	140	40	
Others	125	15	
Weighted CPI			

20 Economics of inequality and poverty

1 Study the data below for Country Y and answer the questions that follow. (HL only)

Income tier	Tax rate (%)
$10,000	0
$10,001–$25,000	10
$25,001–$45,000	20
$45,001 and above	45

a Identify the taxable allowance in Country Y. [1]

b Calculate the amount of tax paid by an individual in Country Y who earns $50,000 a year. [2]

c Calculate the average rate of tax paid by the above individual. [2]

2 An individual earned $25,000 last year and paid $3,250 in indirect taxes. This year, she received a 7.5% pay rise and paid a total of $3,493.75 in indirect taxes.

a Define the term *marginal tax rate*. [2]

b Calculate the marginal rate of indirect tax paid by the individual. [2]

3 The diagram below shows the Lorenz curve for Country Z.

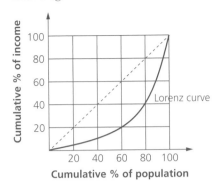

a Outline what the 45-degree line represents for Country Z.   [2]

....

....

....

b With reference to the diagram above, explain the purpose of calculating the Gini coefficient for
Country Z.   [4]

....

....

....

....

....

c Using the diagram, describe the earnings from the third quintile in Country Z.   [2]

....

....

....

4 The data below refer to the income taxes paid by four individuals in Country A.

Individual	Income ($)	Tax paid ($)
A	12,000	600
B	20,000	1,500
C	25,000	2,500
D	45,000	5,625

a Distinguish between regressive and progressive taxes.   [3]

....

....

....

b Use the data to explain whether the tax system in Country A is progressive or regressive. [3]

....

....

....

....

....

....

5 The data below refer to Country H and Country K. The first quintile represents the lowest 20% of income earners while the fifth quintile represents the top 20%.

Country	Percentage of total income earned				
	1st quintile	2nd quintile	3rd quintile	4th quintile	5th quintile
H	6	10	13	23	48
K	9	15	18	22	36

a Explain what the second quintile reveals about income distribution in Countries H and K. [4]

....

....

....

....

....

....

....

b Outline what the fifth quintile reveals about income distribution in Countries H and K. [2]

....

....

....

21 Demand management (demand-side policies) – monetary policy

1 Study the money market diagram below and answer the questions that follow. (HL only)

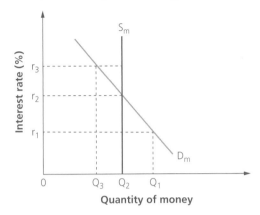

a Define the term *interest rate*. [2]

....

....

....

b Outline why the supply of money (S_m) curve is shown as a vertical line. [2]

....

....

....

c Outline why there would be excess demand for money in the economy at an interest rate of r_1. [2]

....

....

....

2 A commercial bank lends an individual \$350,000 to purchase a house at an interest rate of 3.5%. The inflation rate in the economy is 2%.

a State the nominal interest rate for the individual borrower. [1]

....

b State the real interest rate for the individual borrower. [1]

....

3   The COVID-19 pandemic caused economies across the globe to go into a deep recession. Governments reacted by using expansionary demand-side policies. Using an appropriate AD–AS diagram, explain the use of expansionary monetary policies during an economic downturn.   [4]

4   a   With the aid of a fully labelled diagram, explain how a government can close an inflationary gap in the economy.   [4]

b Define the term *inflationary gap*. [2]

....

....

....

....

....

5 Study the diagram below for Country X and answer the questions that follow.

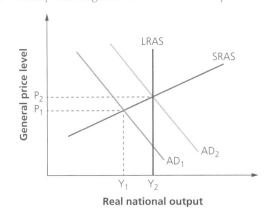

a Identify Country X's real national output in the long run. [1]

....

b Explain whether Country X is experiencing a recessionary gap or an inflationary gap. [2]

....

....

....

....

c Explain **two** methods that Country X can use to close this gap. [4]

....

....

....

....

....

....

d Explain **two** possible causes of an outwards shift of Country X's long run aggregate supply (LRAS) curve. [4]

22 Demand management – fiscal policy (HL only)

1 a The marginal rate of income tax in a country is 35 per cent. Calculate the change in the amount of tax paid by an individual if his or her salary increases from $35,000 to $40,000. [2]

b A worker was paid $35,000 last year and paid $4,800 in indirect taxes. This year, she received a pay rise of 5% and paid a total of $5,010 in indirect taxes. Calculate the marginal rate of indirect tax paid by the individual. [2]

2 In an economy, it is known that the marginal propensity to tax (MPT) = 0.2, the marginal propensity to import (MPM) = 0.15, and the marginal propensity to save (MPS) = 0.1.

a Define the term *Keynesian multiplier*. [2]

b Calculate the change in national income if there is an increase in investment expenditure of $600 million in the economy. [3]

3 An individual in Country Y earns an annual salary of $77,635. The tax brackets in the country are shown below.

Income bracket	Tax band
$0 to $15,000	5%
$15,001 to $35,000	12%
$35,001 to $70,000	15%
$70,001 +	20%

    a Calculate the total amount of tax payable by the individual in Country Y. [2]

    b Calculate the average rate of tax paid by the individual in Country Y. [2]

4 In a particular country, the marginal propensity to consume (MPC) is known to be 0.85.

    a Calculate the country's marginal propensity to withdraw (MPW). [1]

    b Calculate the size of the Keynesian multiplier. [2]

    c Suppose the country's export earnings increases by $200m. Calculate the change in the country's real national income, ceteris paribus. [2]

5 The table below shows the components of last year's nominal gross domestic product (GDP) for Country X.

Component of nominal gross domestic product (GDP)	Value ($bn)
Consumption expenditure	236
Investment expenditure	65
Government expenditure	45
Export earnings	37
Import expenditure	38
Net property income from abroad	-12

a Define the term *nominal gross domestic product* (GDP).　　　　　　　　　　　　　[2]

b Calculate the nominal GDP for Country X using the expenditure method.　　　　　　[2]

c Calculate the nominal gross national income (GNI) for Country X using the expenditure method.　　[2]

d Further data relating to Country X are shown in the table below:

Marginal propensity to import (MPM)	Marginal propensity to tax (MPT)	Marginal propensity to save (MPS)	Marginal propensity to consume (MPC)
0.2	0.15	0.1	0.55

The government of Country X injects $25 million as part of its plans to boost spending in the economy. Calculate the Keynesian multiplier and hence the change in Country X's gross domestic product.　　[2]

Unit 4 The global economy

23 Benefits of international trade and types of trade protection (HL only)

1 Study the diagram below that shows the production possibility curves for two countries, and answer the questions that follow.

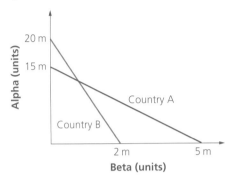

a Calculate the opportunity cost of producing 1 million units of beta for Country A. [2]

....

....

....

b Calculate the opportunity cost of producing 1 million units of alpha for Country B. [2]

....

....

....

c Explain which country should specialize in the output of beta. [2]

....

....

....

2 Refer to the following production possibilities for two countries and answer the questions that follow.

	Fruit (units)	Vegetables (units)
Country K	8,000	0
	0	10,000
Country P	4,000	0
	0	8,000

a Identify which country has the absolute advantage in the production of vegetables. [1]

....

b Explain which country should specialize in the production of fruit. [2]

....

....

c Calculate the opportunity cost of producing 8 units of fruit, in terms of vegetables, for Country P. [2]

....

....

3 The diagram below shows the effects following the imposition of a tariff by Country E's government.

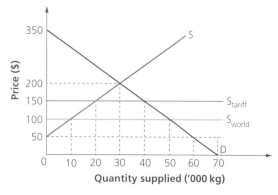

a Calculate the value of consumer surplus before the imposition of the tariff. [2]

....

....

b Calculate the value of producer surplus before the imposition of the tariff. [2]

....

....

c Calculate the consumer surplus after the imposition of the tariff. [2]

....

....

d Calculate the domestic producer surplus after the imposition of the tariff. [2]

....

....

e Calculate the revenue to the government after the imposition of the tariff. [2]

....

....

f Calculate the welfare loss after the imposition of the tariff. [2]

....

....

4 Study the quota diagram below and answer the questions that follow.

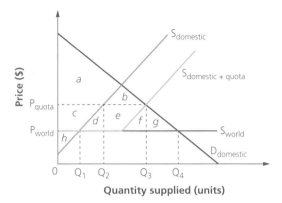

a Identify the consumer surplus before the imposition of the quota. [1]

....

b Identify the producer surplus for domestic firms before the imposition of the quota. [1]

....

c Identify the size of consumer surplus after the imposition of the quota. [1]

....

d Identify the producer surplus for domestic firms after the imposition of the quota. [1]

....

e Identify the welfare loss following the imposition of the quota. [1]

....

5 Study the subsidy diagram below and answer the questions that follow.

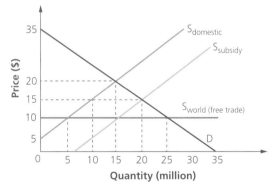

a Calculate the number of imports *before* government intervention. [2]

....

....

....

PHOTOCOPYING PROHIBITED

b Calculate the number of imports *after* government intervention. [2]

c Calculate the cost of the subsidy to the government. [2]

d Calculate the total amount spent by domestic consumers under free trade. [2]

e Calculate the total amount spent on imports by domestic consumers after the imposition of the subsidy. [2]

24 Exchange rates

1 Suppose the exchange rate between the British pound (GBP) and the Hong Kong dollar (HKD) is GBP1 = HKD11.5.

    a Calculate how much it costs a British tourist (in pounds sterling) to buy an iPhone in Hong Kong that is priced at HKD8,000. [2]

    b Suppose that the exchange rate between the Australian dollar (AUD) and the British pound (GBP) is AUD1 = GBP0.55 and between the Hong Kong dollar (HKD) is AUD1 = HKD7.25. Calculate the exchange rate of the GBP against the HKD. [2]

2 Suppose the exchange rate between the British pound (GBP) and the US dollar (USD) is GBP1 = USD1.45.

   a Calculate the price for customers in Britain who buy American cars priced at USD45,500. [2]

   b Calculate the price paid in British pounds by a British tourist spending USD55 for a theme park ticket in Florida, USA. [2]

   c If the US dollar falls against the British pound to USD1 = GBP0.65, calculate the new amount that British tourists have to pay in pounds sterling to enter the theme park. [2]

3 With reference to the diagram below, outline **two** possible reasons for the change in the exchange rate of the British pound (GBP or £) against the Hong Kong dollar (HKD or $). [4]

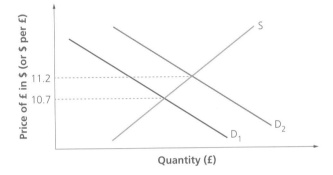

4 Suppose the Canadian dollar (CAD) and Brazilian real (BRL) have an exchange rate of CAD1 = BRL4.36 (i.e. BRL1 = CAD0.23). Use an appropriate diagram and numerical example to explain the effects on the exchange rate following a significant rise in interest rates in Canada, assuming all other factors remain constant.   [4]

5 Although the Chinese government controls the value of its exchange rate, it has been known to allow the yuan (the Chinese currency) to appreciate.

   a Explain what is meant by an appreciation in the value of a currency.   [2]

b Explain **two** likely effects of China's currency appreciation on its exports and imports. [4]

25 Balance of payments

1 The data below show trade figures for Country J in a particular year.

Balance of trade in goods ($m)	
Food, beverages and tobacco	−3,558
Oil	4,305
Finished manufactured goods	−685
Others	−1,886
Balance of trade in services ($m)	
Transportation	−632
Communications	−531
Insurance	1,450
Others	3,776

a Calculate the value on the balance of trade in services for Country J. [2]

b Calculate the balance of trade for Country J. [2]

2 Study the data below for Country K and answer the questions that follow.

Balance of trade for Country K ($bn)	
Exports	85
Goods	57
Services	28
Imports	i
Goods	88
Services	15
Balance of trade in goods	ii
Balance of trade in services	iii
Trade balance	iv

a Define the term *balance of trade in services*. [2]

b Calculate the missing figures in the data above. [4]

3 The table below shows data from Country L's balance of payments.

	$bn		$bn
Exports of goods	235	Net current transfers	−30
Exports of services	320	Net foreign direct investment	65
Imports of goods	−440	Net portfolio investment	38
Imports of services	−235	Capital transfers	26
Net income	20	Transaction in non-produced, non-financial assets	20

a Calculate the value of Country L's current account balance. [2]

b Calculate the value of the financial account for Country L. [2]

c Calculate the value of the capital account for Country L. [2]

....

....

....

d Calculate the value of errors and omissions on the balance of payments for Country L. [2]

....

....

....

4 Sri Lanka is a major exporter of textiles, garments and tea, which combine to account for around 69% of the country's exports. The chart below shows the balance of trade for Sri Lanka from 2011 to 2021.

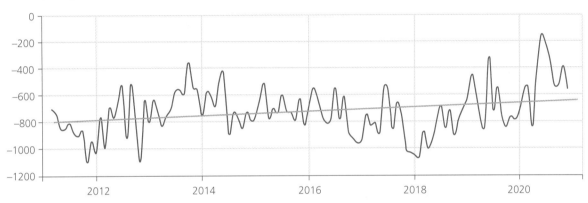

a Define the term *balance of trade*. [2]

....

....

....

....

b Explain **two** possible causes of Sri Lanka's persistent balance of trade deficit as shown in the chart above. [4]

....

....

....

....

....

....

....

5 Kuwait is one of the world's largest net exporters of oil. The chart below shows the ratio of the country's current account balance relative to its gross domestic product (GDP) from 1995 to 2021.

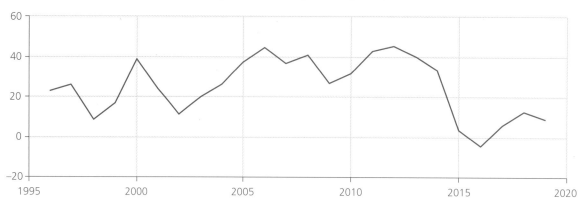

a Define the term *current account surplus*. [2]

....

....

....

b Explain **two** consequences of Kuwait's persistent current account surplus from 1995 to 2021. [4]

....

....

....

....

....

....

....

....

....